RESTORED

A STORY OF LIVES MADE FULL

the book of ruth

ISBN
978-1-998048-03-8 (Paperback)
978-1-998048-10-6 (eBook)

TABLE OF CONTENTS

WELCOME

Most who pick up these pages will already be familiar with the story of *Ruth*. So why read what you already know? Because it is a story, a good story - and good stories deserve repetition. An encyclopedia offers answers for important questions and can then be closed until our next inquiry. But a story carries more than data. It does more than inform, it reveals. A story displays humanity with its strengths and weaknesses. It walks us through common conflicts and delves into hearts and minds. A story is a morning mirror in which we catch our reflection. Regardless of our gender, status, experience or age, there is something in a good story that reaches from the pages into our own lives. That is what the book of *Ruth* does.

But it does more. This is a story written by God. It is historical and accurate. It is about a particular family and a specific people, but it is universal in its scope. The book of *Ruth* describes earthly activity but has the eternal purposes of God as its foundation. Unlike some Bible stories, the book of *Ruth* seems very ordinary. There are no miracles mentioned. No angels show up with grand gestures or announcements. In fact, the voice of God is muted. But His Hand is evident on every page. God is active in the ordinary details of life. In our working, deciding, moving, marrying, burying, through grief or joy, in family and community – God is present. The perception of a distant God is illusion. We may miss the presence of God because we are looking for a "flash and crash" demonstration. But the Sinai lightning and thunder is only one aspect of God's actions. Kingly courts are only a portion of God's stage. *Ruth* tells us that nothing is ordinary or mundane. Your days are a canvas upon which God paints. Amid all that seems small or insignificant in your life, God is at work.

We assume that if God is at work, then our life situation should be delightful. It's a faulty assumption. If this is your first reading of the book of *Ruth*, be warned. It has a troubling start. There is famine, displacement and family tragedy. The flavour of the beginning is bitter. There is grievous loss and disappointment. All of this takes place during troubled times. *Ruth* is the story of one family's struggle amid cultural strife. There is a vacuum of leadership which results in oppression and everyone making up their own way. Chaos. Violence. Lawlessness. The time of the Judges was a cyclical pattern of marauders, heroic deliverance and a return to unrighteousness, which sparked the enemy plunder in the first place. It was clear that no lasting relief would result from human effort or plans. God would have to step in.

Ruth is the story of God's footsteps coming to rescue.

Ruth is a story of redemption. It has been treated like a love story in which a couple meet and get married to live happily ever after. Clearly, it is an account of matrimony which would get repeated to grandchildren over the years. But it is larger than love between a man and a woman. *Ruth* points to God's love for us all. It speaks of a covenant God made with Israel. In His relationship with His people, God said, "I do!" and *Ruth* describes how He does it! God continues His plan of redemption in a time when hope needed to be revived. The theme of redemption fits the largeness of eternal dimensions. But God's redemption is very personal. *Ruth* points to one family and relates how God moved them from hunger to abundance, from bitterness to celebration and from barrenness to a filled cradle. What He does for one family is a seed of hope for us all.

So, if you have not read the Bible story of *Ruth*, set these pages aside, make a cup of coffee or tea and absorb the book. Don't pull it apart in your mind looking for theological principles or Sunday School outlines. Approach it as a child does a bedtime reading. Hear it with your heart. See it in your imagination. Ask "Why?" and don't jump to your own answers. Let the story reveal itself. Let God tell you His story through it. This is a good read for those whose life seems too mundane to matter. For those in a dry spell, where everything is dust and dirt, let this account plant hope for you. When you are surrounded by the chaos of lawless culture, consider this gleam in the darkness. For anyone looking for redemption, consider the way God keeps His Word. Even if all you are looking for is a good story, *Ruth* is a place to start. So, let's begin.

FROM HARD TO HARDER

RUTH 1:1-22

The book of *Ruth* is nestled between the books of Judges and 1 Samuel in our Old Testament. Its placement offers a clue to its purpose. The time of Judges was a nadir in the history of Israel. The days of Moses and Joshua are past. Israel had entered the promised land, but there is no king or prophet to lead the people. Everyone did "what was right in his own eyes" (Judges 21:25, ESV). Before the leadership of Samuel, Saul or David, God used heroes such as Gideon, Debra and Samson to rescue His people from enemy oppression. It worked for a time. The people would align with God's ways, but they soon returned to their own path. The cycle of oppression resumed. In these dark times, many probably asked, "Where is God?" The book of *Ruth* points to a small family struggling with a choice.

Who Should We Cheer For?

Ruth turns a spotlight towards a single family in Israel. *"In the days when the judges ruled there was a famine in the land, and a man of Bethlehem in Judah went to sojourn in the county of Moab, he and his wife and his two sons"* (Ruth 1:1). We are introduced to Elimelech, Naomi and their sons, Mahlon and Chilion. The cast of prime characters in this story will expand to include Ruth and Boaz.

So, who is this book about? Who is our central character? The title suggests that Ruth is the one we should watch. That may be misleading. While Ruth shines in the narrative and there's reason to highlight her words and actions, it is Naomi whose voice is heard loudest. The trajectory of her heart forms the plot of this story. But we should allow the story to unfold on its own and not get too far ahead of ourselves.

Pack up the Donkeys

The story begins with a pivotal decision by Elimelech during a famine. Given the larger context of Judges, we are to understand that the famine was consequence of Israel's disobedience. God allowed the fields to be plundered by enemies. This was not simply punishment, but an enticement from God to return to what is right. Repentance was the proper response to their troubles. Elimelech chose a different course. He decided to pack up his family and go east across the Jordan River to Moab. The text says that they *"remained there"* (Ruth 1:2). In other words, Elimelech wasn't making a short-term decision. He thought their future was in Moab. Elimelech's plan may seem pragmatic. But there is more happening here than a geographic move towards abundance and work. This was not a neutral decision about food. This was a faith decision.

Elimelech was leaving the land of promise for territory that was a historical enemy of Israel. The Moabites descended from Moab, born of incest from Lot and his daughter (Genesis 19:37). The King of Moab once tried to curse Israel through the words of Balaam. When the curses failed, the Moabites induced Israel to idolatry through intermarriage (Numbers 22:5,25:1). In other words, Moab was not a place to settle. Elimelech chose to live and raise his family in an immoral and idolatrous culture, hostile to Israel. We can sympathize with Elimelech's sense of desperation to feed his family, but rather than trusting God, he made his own way. He left Bethlehem for Moab. He is sowing seeds that will reap trouble.

From Little to Nothing

Very quickly in the story, we are told that Elimelech dies (Ruth 1:3). Was this God's judgement? The scripture is silent about the cause or reason for Elimelech's death. It seems to have happened promptly after their move. Despite our questions about Elimelech, the narrative shifts to Naomi. She followed her husband to Moab and is now a widow in a foreign land. She has two sons to raise and care for. A widow's plight is difficult in any situation, but Naomi has no property or male protection, living among a foreign culture. Naomi's life has become hard. Naomi chose wives for her sons from Moab. They married Orpah and Ruth. After 10 years, the sons still had no children with their wives. Naomi had meager hope for the future. A dead husband and barren wombs – both were suggestions of God's displeasure. Naomi's darkness was about to get darker. Mahlon and Chilion died. Again, we have no details or explanation, simply the sudden silence of loss, leaving a trio of widows. Naomi's life has moved from hard to harder. Imagine their plight, sorrow and confusion. Their husbands are dead. They have no means of sustaining their lives. There are no children born to point to a hopeful future. Grief, fear and desperation have coloured their lives. If the story had a soundtrack, it would be in a minor key – but the music begins to change.

Empty and Bitter

After 10 years and so much loss, Naomi decides to return home. She has heard news that the famine in Israel is receding. God is bringing harvests to the fields of Bethlehem. "The House of Bread" is replenished. When Naomi chooses to return to Judah, her daughters-in-law initially decide to go with her. Either from nurtured love or a sense of family loyalty, they want to accompany Naomi. Naomi seeks to dissuade them. *"...Go, return each of you to her mother's house. May the Lord deal kindly with you, as you have dealt with the dead and with me. The Lord grant that you may find* rest, each of you in the house of her husband!..." (Ruth 1:8-9). Naomi recognizes the kind loyalty of Orpah and Ruth, but she believes that their future is with their own family and kinsmen. She prays that God might give them new husbands and reminds them that there is no potential in a future with her (Ruth 1:11). It's important that we recognize the cultural context. When Naomi says that there is no hope for a husband for her, nor for Orpah or Ruth through her, she is not talking about romance. She is not talking of schoolgirls daydreaming of a future prince. Naomi is speaking of survival. The life and sustenance of a widow was demanding, with little hope for a future. When Naomi looks down the road, she sees bitterness. She concludes that *"...the Hand of the Lord has gone out against me"* (Ruth 1:13). Her days will be bleak, so she urges her daughters-in-law to find a better future elsewhere.

Called by God

Orpah responds to Naomi's logic and returns to her people. But Ruth makes a different decision. She resists Naomi's persuasion and rebuts her words with a pledge, *"...For where you go I will go, and where you lodge I will lodge. Your people shall be my people, and your God my God"* (Ruth 1:16). It's hard to know where her commitment came from. She embraces Naomi's journey, home, people and God. She ties herself to Naomi's future. She promises to be buried with Naomi and prays for God to take her life if anything less than death should separate them (Ruth 1:17). Clearly there was a committed relationship between the women, but there is more going on than family loyalty and appreciation.

Ruth was pledging her allegiance to a new land, new culture, new home and new God. Her decision is remarkable considering her situation. Like Naomi, she has lost her husband. Like Naomi, she has no children. Ruth has experienced the same struggle of widowhood and sees the same prospects that Naomi sees. Yet Ruth embraces it. This is a faith decision. God is calling this woman and she responds with, "Yes." At this point in the story, Ruth may not have understood her actions in that light. Ruth's understanding of Jehovah will expand as the story unfolds. But like Moses, Rahab, Samuel and Esther, the Voice which calls and the Hand which moves, is God's. He is active in the details and decisions of our days.

Amid scarcity and tragedy, God is at work providentially.

A Bitter Void

When these two women return to Bethlehem, there is a buzz. Family and friends had not seen Naomi in over a decade. She returns without husband or children, accompanied only by a Moabite daughter-in-law. At first, people aren't sure of her identity, *"Is this Naomi?"* The hard years had been traced on her face, but the imprint went all the way to her heart. The name Naomi means "pleasant." She refused to be called that any longer. She insists that she be called Mara, which means "bitter" (Ruth 1:20). She says, *"...for the Almighty has dealt very bitterly with me. I went away full, and the Lord has brought me back empty. Why call me Naomi, when the Lord has testified against me and the Almighty has brought calamity upon me?"* (Ruth 1:20-21). Naomi attributes her troubles to God and has become embittered because of it. It's true that Naomi's response to the scars of life is not like Job's or Joseph's. Job blesses the Lord in severe loss (Job 1:21). Joseph sees the goodness of God through the intentions of evil (Genesis 50:20). All Naomi sees is her emptiness, and she wears it like a nametag. But the story is not over. In fact, Naomi returns to Bethlehem at the beginning of barley harvest (Ruth 1:22). Maybe emptiness and bitterness won't have the last word.

TIME TO REFLECT

Good stories not only stay with us, but they speak to our lives. That is specifically true with biblical stories written by the Spirit of God. Take a few moments to consider your own life in reflection of this first chapter.

- Are there times you think your life is too small or mundane to matter to God? What does the story of Ruth suggest for your routine days, or even troubled times?

- Think of a time when a decision you made didn't turn out the way you expected. Did God turn that into good? How? What did you learn in the pains of a bad decision?

- Naomi blamed God for the troubles of life. Ruth embraced God in the troubles of life. In these days, which reflection is yours?

GOD IS IN THE DETAILS

RUTH 2:1-23

Serendipity

The word looks like it belongs in a Mary Poppin's movie. It sounds cheery and bubbles off the tongue. And the sound matches the meaning. The dictionary defines "serendipity" as the discovery of something pleasant. It's a $20 bill on the sidewalk, or an abandoned umbrella against a wall, just as it starts to rain. You've experienced serendipity and told the story with a smile. But do you rely on it? Are the good things in life happenstance? Are we left to the tides of chance for our provision, guidance and happiness? The second chapter of *Ruth* turns our heads from "luck" to a different direction.

The Bi-Focal of Faith

The first chapter of *Ruth* ends with Naomi singing a solo of self-pity. *"Call me bitter! God has been hard against me."* She has the evidence to back that up. Her husband and sons have died. She is left alone with her daughter-in-law, Ruth. Ruth exudes the meaning of her name — "friend." Her loyalty and commitment were appreciated, but it still wasn't enough to illuminate the dark places of Naomi's spirit. Naomi remains "Mara." Pleasant turned bitter. So, what is the distinction between these two, despite having suffered similar losses?

A central question of life is, "How do you see God?" Our perspective of God will inform our thinking, feeling and actions. We all have a lens through which we view Him. Our perception is shaped by our personality, experience and nurturing. Ultimately, a right perception is formed by the teaching and truth of God's Word. God reveals Himself. He invites us how to understand Him accurately. Naomi didn't. It seems evident that Naomi saw God as someone "who takes." God took her home, her husband, her sons and her future. She says that she left Bethlehem full and returned empty (Ruth 1:21).

Ruth sees God through a different lens. Ruth views God as One worthy of trust. Her actions prove it. She embraces the people of God, the land of God, the worship of God (Ruth 1:16-17). Ruth hands God her future. Ruth does this despite the hardships of her own loss and the pessimism of Naomi's spirit. Through all of this, Ruth sees God as "One who gives." She sees God as a reason for hope. While one woman responds with bitterness, the other responds with faith. Which one "sees" God better? Back to the story.

Field of Gleans

The demands of life compel action. Without a means of support, Naomi and Ruth still have to eat. Ruth volunteered to glean for food (Ruth 2:2). Gleaning was an Old Testament practice stipulated by God. The Law required that a landowner not harvest every square inch of their fields. They were to leave the borders and corners of the crop for the poor (Leviticus 19:9-10). If a sheaf was dropped or forgotten, they were not to retrieve it. They were forbidden to go over a field a second time, trying to get every kernel into the barn (Deuteronomy 24:19). Gleaning did three things. It testified that the land belonged to God. It put a restraint on the greed of landowners, and it provided a resource of food for the poor, widows and orphans. Those in need were allowed to gather the remnants of the fields. That is not to suggest that gleaning was easy or always safe. It was highly competitive, and landowners didn't always take kindly to those who enjoyed a harvest they didn't plant. It may be that Naomi was too frail for the hard work, so Ruth took the initiative. It was time for the barley harvest, and workers were already in the fields. Ruth had no inkling of where to begin. She had no history here nor friends to guide her. She probably scouted the fields and saw gleaners working in the wake of labourers, like gulls following a fishing trolley. Ruth joined in. The text says, *"...she happened to come to the part of the field belonging to Boaz..."* (Ruth 2:3). A random chance? Ruth blended in as she could, a Moabite widow among the poor of Israel. She didn't go un-noticed. Boaz saw her and approached.

Just the Right Place

The field belonged to Boaz, who was also from Bethlehem. He was of Elimelech's clan, a relative. Boaz saw this young woman and asked his foreman about her. It was reported that she was Ruth, Naomi's daughter-in-law, and she had worked hard from sunrise, with scarcely a break. Boaz didn't need any more information. Bethlehem was a small town where news splashed everywhere. He had heard of Naomi's return, and of Ruth who accompanied her. He admired Ruth's choices and wanted to extend security, comfort and abundance. Boaz showed her hospitality. He assured her that she could follow his workers, and no one would harm her. She was allowed to drink the well water drawn by the workers. She could even pull barley from the sheaves which were already gathered. He instructed his men to drop a little bit extra on the ground. The epitome of kindness came at mealtime. Boaz invited Ruth to sit and eat with his workers. The other gleaners must have stared. This was way beyond requirements and custom. Boaz became Ruth's protection and provision.

Under His Wings

Ruth was grateful, but confused. *"...Why have I found favour in your eyes, that you should take notice of me, since I am a foreigner?"* (Ruth 2:10). Boaz told her that he had heard of her commitment and courage. He was impressed that Ruth would not abandon her mother-in-law and had embraced a new land, culture and people. Most of all, Boaz applauded her faith. *"The Lord repay you for what you have done, and a full reward be given you by the Lord, the God of Israel, under whose wings you have come to take refuge!"* (Ruth 2:12). Boaz is not simply responding to the abundance of Ruth's kindness. He points to the pledge of trust Ruth made, "Your God shall be my God." Ruth has made Jehovah as her refuge. *"He will cover you with His pinions, and under His wings you will find refuge..."* (Psalm 91:4). Ruth believed that, even before it was written. It explains the motivation for her choice to leave Moab. It unmasks the mystery of her hope, despite her own pain. It fortifies her endurance and efforts to care for Naomi. None of this was simply the product of her personality or cheery disposition. Ruth had faith that God is a Refuge she could trust. So, she trusted Him.

Glint of Hope for Naomi

At the end of the day, Ruth had gleaned about 14 kilograms of barley. She carried it home to Naomi, who must have been surprised. There was more than enough barley to sustain them. They could sell the surplus. As Ruth shared the left-over food provided by Boaz, Naomi grilled her. "Where did you find all this food? Whose field did you glean at?" Ruth was excited to explain her day, and when she mentioned Boaz, Naomi stopped her. For the first time in the story, you hear praise from the lips of Naomi. *"...May [Boaz] be blessed by the Lord, whose kindness has not forsaken the living or the dead!..."* (Ruth 2:20). She is grateful to Boaz, but praises the Lord. God has not forgotten His kindness for those who have passed, nor for those who have survived. It is the first crack we see in her bitter heart. It is the first glimmer of hope she voices. Perhaps her emptiness is not permanent. God has remembered His kindness.

Naomi is delighted with the generous way Boaz treated Ruth. She repeats what Boaz had told Ruth. "Follow his workers. Stay in his fields." Naomi's eye is not simply on the barley. She knows that Boaz is a relative, one who is qualified to change their future. Boaz could be their redeemer. But that is yet to come in the story.

Providence of God

Remember serendipity? The idea that occasionally, we fall upon something good and helpful. Is that what this chapter is about? Clearly there was a connection of time and place that proved to be beneficial for Naomi and Ruth. Ruth happened upon the right field. The field owner happened to be kind and generous. Boaz happened to be related to Elimelech. The likelihood of all these things coordinating just right is beyond the realm of coincidence. None of this is chance. All of it is providence. The Bible teaches that God is in control. He rules over everything. In fact, Jesus has His grip on that which is large or small, spiritual or secular, delightful or harsh (Colossians 1:7). And while God moves subtly through our ordinary life, without fanfare or Hollywood production, He is active. Naomi doesn't see this as luck. She proclaimed that God has remembered! God has been moving people and planets, family and farmers, barley and Boaz to bring this about. He has timed Naomi's return when the crops are ripe. He has used the loyalty, kindness, labour and faith of Ruth to arrange a pivotal meeting. God's Hand is the cause of all things, and therefore, there is reason for hope.

Frankly, if we wait for serendipity to happen, there's no reason for confidence. Serendipity doesn't know your name!

God knows you. He sees your days in all their detail. He loves you with an eternal heart.

He is working all things together for a glorious purpose (Romans 8:28-30). The purposes of God are not void of struggle or pain. The ways of God are not always obvious. The schedule of God can't be measured by a stopwatch. The reasons of God may remain a mystery. But His promises are true. His heart is holy. His hand is mighty. His wisdom is perfect. His love cannot be denied. We do not rely upon chance. We rest in the care of the One who holds this universe together by the power of His Word (Heb.1:3). We need not ricochet through life hoping to bump into something good. Like Ruth, we can take shelter under His wings.

TIME TO REFLECT

• Consider a time when a seeming coincidence proved to be the providence of God. What happened? How did God work that for good?

• Review your day. Can you spot evidence of God's Hand? What if they are hidden from you; is God absent? How have you had to live by faith today?

• Naomi is beginning to see a reason for hope. Where do you need a renewed spark of hope? How will that happen?

III

<u>WINGS OF REFUGE</u>

RUTH 3:1-18

First Dates

Parents eventually hear this question from their children, "How did you start to date?" They want to know how mom and dad met, what their first date was like and who gathered courage to take the initiative. So, we tell them of a dinner out, a church youth function or a casual walk through a park. They hear of sweaty palms and awkward dialogue, but also of goosebumps and hopes for a future. We tell the children our story, not simply to satisfy curious minds or to offer a template for their own courtship. Our story is about how God began a beginning - the start of a relationship that became the start of a marriage and family. How would Ruth and Boaz answer that question? How will their story be passed down to Obed, Jesse and David? The third chapter of *Ruth* records the details for us.

Jewish Real Estate 101

Naomi has a plan. She has learned that Ruth has been gleaning in fields owned by Boaz. Boaz is a relative of Naomi's deceased husband. He therefore qualifies as a "kinsman redeemer" for them (Ruth 2:20). We will need to pause our story for a brief tutorial on real estate dealings in Jewish culture. As technical as that is, it's essential to understand Naomi's plan.

God owns all the land there is! *"The earth is the Lord's and the fullness thereof..."* (Psalm 24:1). While property may be deeded to someone, it all belongs to God. When Israel entered the land of "milk and honey," God graced to each of the tribes an allotment of land. That land was to stay with the tribe and their descendants. In that way, the land would never be lost. In an agrarian culture, land is life! If you lose your land, you lose the resources of life and your heritage. Eventually, a tribe could lose its place and identity. Even if someone sold their property out of need or desperation, the land returned to the original family in the Year of Jubilee (Leviticus 25).

Property was to be passed down to the eldest son of a family in each tribe. If there were no sons, a daughter would inherit the land. But Naomi had no sons or daughters. We assume that when Elimelech left Bethlehem for Moab, he sold his property to another. Someone else was farming property that Naomi needed for a home and income. She had claim to it, in Elimelech's name. She could wait for the Year of Jubilee for her property to return, but that only happened every 50 years! We don't know when in the cycle Naomi returned to Bethlehem, but she couldn't wait. There was a way for the property to return to Naomi now. It involved a "kinsman redeemer."

A kinsman redeemer was a relative who could set things right. He could seek justice for a family that has suffered injury. He could take on debilitating debts that a household accrued and set the family free. He could restore property that has been sold and return it to the original owner (Leviticus 25:25). Obviously then, a kinsman redeemer had to be a relative of wealth, authority and compassion. Boaz met all those conditions. He was a "worthy" man in character and reputation (Ruth 2:1). He had riches and demonstrated kindness. But he could do more.

The Best Man Becomes the Groom

As kinsman redeemer, Boaz could buy back Elimelech's land and restore it to Naomi. But still, she would remain a widow, who was caring for another widow — Ruth. They needed more than just fields. They needed family for a future. God had provided a way for a kinsman redeemer to do that as well. God stipulated that if a man dies leaving a widow with no children, then a brother of the deceased could marry the widow. Their children would then be considered the descendants of the deceased. His name, property and heritage would not end by his death (Deuteronomy 25:5). Acting as a kinsman redeemer in this manner was not compulsory, but to refuse was a mark of shame. A man of character would fulfill his responsibility. Boaz could act as kinsman redeemer for Elimelech's property, but he also qualified to redeem the family's future by marriage. He was a relative, probably widowed. There is no mention of Boaz's wife in the story. Having checked all the boxes, if he was willing to buy back the property and even marry and have children, then Elimelech's heritage would not be lost. Naomi and Ruth would have a future. How could this be arranged? Naomi had a plan. Return to the story.

Date Night

If Boaz were willing, who should he marry? He could take Naomi as his bride, but she was past the age of having children. Having a family was the whole point here. Obviously, Ruth would be the one to marry Boaz and continue the line of Elimelech by her children. Ruth's prospects of finding a husband on her own were dimmed because she was from Moab. Moabites had a shady reputation in Israel. Even if Ruth found a husband, their descendants wouldn't continue Elimelech's heritage and property. Neither Ruth nor the prospective husband were blood relatives of Elimelech. The only reasonable course was for Ruth and Boaz to marry. Naomi decided to put that course into action.

Out of concern for both of their futures, Naomi tells Ruth to rummage through the closet and put on her best outfit. She was to bath and anoint herself with perfumes. Naomi knows where Boaz will be this evening. It is threshing season, a time when the harvest is winnowed to grain. Boaz would be there protecting the grain from being pilfered. Naomi counsels Ruth to not make her presence known to Boaz until after he has had his fill of food and drink. When he lies down, Ruth is to uncover his feet, and wait for guidance from Boaz. Ruth agrees. In the dark of night, once Boaz is full and "merry," he lies on the pile of grain (Ruth 3:7). Ruth comes up to him softly, uncovers his feet and silently waits.

Hanky-Panky?

Once again, we need to put the story on pause. What is going on here? The details of Naomi's plan seem strange at best and morally questionable at worst. A rendezvous in the dark. Uncovering "feet." The story carries a bit of innuendo. It was known that prostitutes visited the threshing floors of field hands. The phrase "feet" is used in other places of the Old Testament as a euphemism for the lower private parts of the body. Ruth is told to dress "to please" and Boaz is described as "merry" after drinking. A reader wonders what is happening. Perhaps we are meant to.

Ruth is a Moabite. Jewish readers would know the story and connect the dots. In Genesis 19, Lot is drunk, and his two daughters go to him at night. They have no husband nor children, no potential for a future. They decide to become pregnant by their father. It was an immoral plan out of desperation. The older daughter gives birth to a son and names him "Moab," the father of all Moabites. The parallels with this account in *Ruth* are obvious. A drunk man at night visited by a woman without husband or child, looking for a future – and the woman is a Moabite. You can almost hear Jewish readers thinking, "Here we go again. True to form, Ruth is a Moabite, immoral and devious." But that is not the case. The story doesn't allow for it.

Ruth and Boaz are not immoral. Nothing happens sexually between them. Throughout the whole story, the character of both Boaz and Ruth is unshakable. Boaz ensures that Ruth's reputation is guarded (Ruth 3:14). This is not gossip to be whispered in secret. This is an account of honourable actions and redemption.

A Marriage Proposal

In the night, Boaz is startled awake to find Ruth. When he discovers who it is, he wonders what she wants. Ruth is clear, *"...Spread your wings over your servant, for you are a redeemer"* (Ruth 3:9). Ruth uses the same phrase Boaz said to her from chapter 2:12. Even as Ruth sought refuge under God's wings, she asks Boaz to become her refuge as a redeemer. She is asking for the Levitate marriage of Deuteronomy 25:5. She invites Boaz to redeem her losses and those of Naomi by marriage and children. Boaz understands her. He is not affronted by the request, nor the method of it. He sees this as an act of kindness, a kindness directed towards Naomi and himself (Ruth 3:10). He knows there are younger men of closer connection she could have approached. Ruth has already impressed him by her character and faith, so with no delay, he agrees. He promises to speak in the morning to a relative who is closer, first in line to redeem the family. If he will not redeem Ruth and Naomi, then Boaz will.

In the morning, Boaz discreetly sent Ruth on her way (Ruth 3:14-15). He wants nothing to colour her reputation and their prospective marriage. He does one more thing. Boaz fills the cloak of Ruth with barley and sends her back to Naomi. When Naomi asks how the proposal went, Ruth quotes Boaz, *"...You must not go back empty-handed to your mother-in-law"* (Ruth 3:17). Boaz was going to redeem the life of both Ruth and Naomi. Naomi was sure that Boaz would not rest until the matter was settled (Ruth 3:18). The years of emptiness and loss were coming to an end. That which was bitter could become pleasant once more.

Providential People

For Ruth and Boaz, it was a good story to pass onto their children. But it is more than a romantic anecdote. This is a record of redemption. It is the drama of God's intervention in our lives and the ways He brings providential people to us. People of providence are those that God ushers into our days that become pivotal. They guide, protect and sustain us on the path God has for us.

> ## God has a plan for every one of our lives. We are His workmanship created in Christ Jesus.

We are to do the works that God has prepared for us (Ephesians 2:10). It is the manner of God to provide people to help us walk in the path He has ordained. For Paul, there is a Barnabas. For Moses, a Joshua. For David, a Jonathan. For Esther, a Mordecai. For Naomi, a Ruth and for Ruth, a Boaz.

Consider the providential people in your life. It may be a parent who held you together when you were falling apart. It may be a teacher who saw more potential in you than was obvious to others. It could have been a stranger whose brief word or kind gesture gave you hope. Perhaps a Bible teacher or pastor shaped your soul towards godliness and service. Whoever it has been or will be, providential people are the Hands and Voice of God which set our life in the right direction. They are people of hope, provided by God.

TIME TO REFLECT

- Naomi risked putting her life and Ruth's in the pathway of God's redemption. She didn't know how it would turn out. Think of a time you boldly trusted God to rescue you. Why did you risk it? How did it turn out?

- The account of Boaz and Ruth demonstrates righteous actions despite raised eyebrows. How can you act morally today, despite the cultural current pushing you in the other direction?

- Consider the providential people God has brought into your life. What impactful grace did God bring you through them? Have you thanked God and them? Is God inviting you to be a providential person for others? How?

IV

<u>EMPTINESS MADE FULL</u>

RUTH 4:1-22

Bartering in Bethlehem

Have you ever been in a street market and haggled for something you wanted? The price tag is just a suggestion and invites a dance of negotiation. The vendor boasts of the item's quality. You point out its flaws. Both sides are so adamant that you begin to wonder why the vendor would let it go, or why you would want it! The bartering can be loud and even seem aggressive. But both parties understand. This is part of the process to set a fair price. The negotiations are successful when the vendor smiles at his profit and you leave with the deal of the day!

The last chapter of *Ruth* begins with a similar scene. Some may be offended by it. "They are arguing over Ruth like she was a rug or a clay pot!" Our western sensitivities are misplaced. The negotiations are not about Ruth as property. She is not being bought or sold. The conversation is about legal rights and a family future. Who will take up the rightful role as "redeemer" for Ruth and Naomi? It is a discussion that Naomi and Ruth asked for. Their future depends on who will do what is right.

Sealed by a Shoe

True to his word, Boaz begins the process of redemption. He knows that there is a closer relative of Elimelech, who has the first right of redemption. If he concedes his right, then Boaz can marry Ruth and purchase the land of Elimelech's heritage. This needs to be legal and done in the presence of witnesses. So, Boaz goes to the place for transactions – the town gate. It was customary for matters of law, social impact or even gossip to take place at the comings and goings of a town. Boaz plants himself at the gate until he sees the relative he is looking for. He invites him to sit and then invites ten other town elders to join them. The relative would quickly recognize that something bigger than "tea and chat" was taking place.

Boaz begins to speak of Naomi, not Ruth (Ruth 4:3). The issue at hand was Naomi's claim to property, held by her deceased husband. Boaz speaks of Naomi selling the property. In our mind, we think of her becoming rich with the equity. But that's not what is happening. Someone else currently owns the land and Naomi is presenting her rightful claim to it. She is inviting a relative to buy the land in her name. She won't get money. She will get the land as a home for her future. The nearest relative jumps at the opportunity (Ruth 4:4). It may be that he wanted to increase his holdings, or perhaps he wanted to look like he was doing what is right before the ten elders and gathered crowd. Once the relative agrees, Boaz offers a reminder. *"...The day you buy the field from the hand of Naomi, you also acquire Ruth the Moabite..."* (Ruth 4:5). The relative would take the responsibility of providing a husband and children for Ruth, to perpetuate Elimelech's line. That was more than the relative wanted. He was concerned about endangering his own family's inheritance. He had demonstrated his good intention before the town and at the same time, protected his own family heritage. He could let this go without public shame. Boaz stepped up. He proclaimed his intentions to not only redeem the property for Naomi, but also to marry Ruth. The legal transaction was confirmed by the giving of a sandal (Ruth 4:7). Boaz would step on the new property with this sandal and claim it as his own.

Naomi Has a Baby

The townspeople bore witness to the legality of the deal. They then burst into a blessing for the family. They prayed that the marriage of Boaz and Ruth would be as prolific as Rachael and Leah, whom the twelve tribes of Israel claimed as their mother. They prayed that "worthy" Boaz (Ruth 2:1) would be seen as being worthy in all the land. They asked God to bless the offspring of Ruth, even as He blessed the offspring of Tamar, who also gave birth through Judah as a "kinsman redeemer" (Genesis 38). God heard their prayers. Boaz married Ruth and she gave birth to a son (Ruth 4:13). Previously, Ruth had been married for ten years without conception. God smiled with mercy upon the marriage of Boaz and Ruth.

We should take care to hear what the women say at the birth of Ruth's child. The women of town look to Naomi and say, *"...blessed be the Lord, who has not left you this day without a redeemer..."* (Ruth 4:14). The word "redeemer" has a trio of referents. The redeemer is Boaz, who bought back their land and took up a bride. The redeemer is the child, who will be *"...a restorer of life and a nourisher of your old age..."* (Ruth 4:15). And of course, the redeemer is God. *"The Lord has not left you this day without a redeemer!"* Naomi takes the boy upon her knees and cares for him (Ruth 4:16). The proclamation at the birth of Ruth's boy is this, *"...A son has been born to Naomi..."* (Ruth 4:17).

Our God of Restoration

Our minds go back to the beginning of this story. During famine, the family goes to Moab. Naomi suffers the death of her husband. She arranges wives for her two boys – but then, they both die without any children. When Naomi and Ruth return to Bethlehem,

Naomi insists that people call her "bitter." She has been squeezed and emptied of the blessings of life. God's hand has been hard against her. There are whispers of hope as the story continues. Ruth exceeds expectations. Boaz generously feeds them. A potential "redeemer" agrees to Ruth's proposal. There is a marriage and a birth. Just before the curtain comes down on the story, the choral sings, "Naomi has had a boy!" The story ends with God's restoration of life for Naomi.

This is a story of hope. It doesn't skip over the tragedy and struggle of life. It honestly presents the despair and bitterness tasted by many. While God never says a word, performs a miracle or displays His presence, He is active in the mundane. He rules the routine. Our God of providence is protecting and providing. He restores the land, provides a family but most crucial of all, He revives hope. The faith of Ruth was not disappointed. The God she embraced was a Refuge for her. The faith of Naomi was renewed. God proved to be a Restorer of life for her.

Naomi and You

Good stories intersect our own lives. We can see ourselves in their reflection. There may have been parts of this story that resonated with you. Have you ever felt "hard done by" with God? Do you think that God takes more than He gives? Has life overwhelmed you like a smothering blanket? No one denies that there are "winter seasons" in our life. But if you have lost hope of "spring", this story speaks of the restoration of God. God can be trusted as a Refuge. He promises more, not less. He enriches our lives to the full. The fullness can't simply be measured by an accountant, the number of "likes" on our posts or the rewards we hang on our walls. But in every situation we face, we can be filled with hope and taste the joy of knowing that God is not blind or deaf to us. He is present and orchestrating our life towards His good purpose. The good purpose of God is for His glory and our fulfillment. That brings us to the last word on this story.

Microscope and Telescope

The baby born to Ruth and laid in Naomi's lap is named Obed. His family tree is spelled out for us (Ruth 4:16-22). Obed would be a gateway of future blessing. After Naomi, Ruth and Boaz have passed on, Obed would marry and have a child named Jesse. Jesse would become the father of David. David would become King of Israel. The darkness of the time of Judges would be replaced by the glory of David's reign. The glory of his throne would be even more glorious than any could imagine. David is the ancestor of Jesus Christ, the Son of David.

The Messiah comes to us through a story of famine, hardship and death. God uses a heart made bitter, a heart that sought refuge and a heart that was worthy. God harmonized the ordinary with extra ordinary purpose. He does this for restoration, that which is found in Jesus. In Jesus, we find the restoration of death to life, sinners to saints, broken lives made richly full and creation renewed as God's Kingdom.

Both microscopes and telescopes improve our vision. The microscope reveals what is small. In telescopes we see the vastness of galaxies. We often use a micro lens in our lives. We see the minutia, the details of that which is close to us. We see it well, but we are missing a bigger picture. We need a macro perspective that takes in the grander scale of time and space. Of course, infinity and eternity are beyond our vision. It's easier for us to just see what is in front of us. So, we live by faith. We trust the goodness, wisdom and power of our God. We rely upon His providence. We yield our questions to Him. We place our pains into His Hands. We make Him our refuge.

The story of Ruth is microscopic. One family in a specific time. Despite its smallness, it is not unimportant. Quite the opposite. God is doing something very large through that which is small. There is grandeur hidden under the daily grind. God is in the details of our lives. Like Ruth, Boaz and eventually Naomi, we learn to not imprison our sight to just what we can see.

We set our eyes upon God and know that there is more going on in the heavens than we can ever perceive on this earth.

TIME TO REFLECT

- Where has God restored an emptiness in your life? Think of it and thank Him.

- Is there an unmet emptiness that wears on your soul? How can you live by faith in this area?

- Consider a time when God was doing something large in your life, that you didn't see at first. How can remembering that inform your future?

FINALLY...

<u>ONE MORE STORY</u>

The introduction suggested that we can often see ourselves in a good story. Since good stories touch what is common among us, we readily recognize our own traits and truths. Here is a smaller story to back that up. A Canadian pastor writes to **Back to the Bible Canada** with this connection to the story of *Ruth*.

"I've been a shepherd of God's flock for several decades across Canada. This calling of God has enriched me and my family. The blessings of God are broader than any specific path, but in this avenue, I found meaning and purpose. Several times over a coffee, I have been asked this question. 'So, was you father a pastor too?' The question assumes that what they see in their pastor must have come from a long Christian heritage. I smile because I know the truth.

My parents met and married shortly after WWII. My dad had served in the Canadian navy and returned to a small Ontario town. I see photos of mom and dad from that time and catch the smiling eyes they had for each other. They both came from rather large families. Dad had 9 siblings, for a family of 12. Mom exceeded that with 11 siblings, bringing their household to 14 under one roof! So, I have enough aunts and uncles and cousins to fill a small stadium. But that would never happen. In fact, I have never met most of them and know only one or two by sight.

Both families were fractured by fault lines of their own making. My mother's home was torn by tensions and disagreements. Her own mother had been abandoned by a philandering husband. When my maternal grandmother remarried, some of the siblings could not accept the colour of her new husband's skin. Arguments. Accusations. Distance. Divisions. Grudges that hardened over time. It's useless to investigate who was wrong or right. Regardless, it resulted in a family that was in pieces. The home professed faith, but that simply meant that they knew a favourite hymn or two. Jesus seemed largely absent.

My father's family had its own set of challenges. His father drank. Phone calls had to scout the home to see if grandpa was sober before a family visit. The children — all 12 of them, my dad included, had a rough reputation. I've had strangers recognize my last name and mention that they would cross the street if they saw my dad coming. There were family secrets to cover up unwanted pregnancies. Some of my uncles spent time in prison. While the blows were different, my dad's family was also broken. It was another home of conflict and anger. It lacked even the facade of faith.

So by His great wisdom, God decided to put my parents together, both of them having a pretty distorted picture of what family should be. By almost any earthly measure, they would surely re-create the families they came from. But God intervened. Both mom and dad came to faith in Jesus. They began a new life and family. They didn't do it perfectly, no one does. But God's healing grace was greater than the injury of sin. They raised four children, including me. All have come to faith in Jesus. Half of us have dedicated our lives to service for His Kingdom. All of us have tasted the compassion and kindness of God.

The point is simple. When God redeemed my parents, He was changing more lives than the obvious. He was redeeming my future and that of my siblings and even future generations. So now, what had been - wasn't repeated. The patterns of the past did not predict our tomorrows. Like showers upon a desert, grace flowed into our lives. Now there are four generations of faith. Great grandparents, grandparents, children and grandchildren. None of us would profess to be pristine. All of us lean into faith and trust God's Hand upon our lives. Jesus has made the difference.

No, I don't come from a long lineage of faith in my family. But I do come from a God who intervenes in the shadows and darkness with His love and mercy.

I come from a Saviour who stepped into our world to set it right.

While there remains more to rectify, this truth is undeniable: God cleanses what sin has stained. God straightens what sin has distorted. God puts in what sin had taken out."

May His Name Be Praised!

NOTES:

NOTES:

NOTES:

Milton Keynes UK
Ingram Content Group UK Ltd.
UKHW050742040324
438876UK00008B/182